Hello,

Thank you for purchasing my first coloring book! Each illustration includes gratitude and mindfulness prompts to help you relax, reflect, and enjoy coloring cozy moments.
I hope it will be the first in a series of creative and inspiring books.

I hope you will enjoy creating your unique book of colorful cozy moments.

Warmly,
Eve Taite

Tips for an Enjoyable Coloring Experience

1. Color using alcohol markers or colored pencils.

2. Insert a blank sheet behind each page to avoid ink bleeding through

UNWIND IN
COZY GIRL MOMENTS:
A COLORING BOOK WITH MINDFULNESS
& GRATITUDE PROMPTS

This Book Belongs to:

_____

Cozy Textures: Focus on the textures around you – your favorite jumper, a soft pillow, or a warm blanket. How do these textures contribute to your sense of comfort?

Bakery Delights: Recall a favorite baked treat. What memories or feelings does it bring for you?

Embrace the Present: Reflect on what you appreciate about this moment. What thoughts or feelings arise when you focus on the here and now?

Gratitude for Solitude: While you're enjoying a peaceful moment alone, think about what you appreciate regarding solitude and the space it gives you for self-reflection

Nature Connection: If you're enjoying a cozy scene outdoors, take a second to notice the natural world. What elements contribute to your sense of coziness?

Savor the Senses: Take a moment to focus on the sensations around you. What do you see, hear, smell, feel, and taste in this cozy moment?

Moments of Connection: Think about a recent conversation with a friend or family member that made you feel warm inside. What about that interaction are you thankful for?

Inspirational Crafts: Think about a handmade item that holds sentimental value. What does it mean to you, and who or what inspired it?

Memory Lane: Recall a childhood memory that evokes coziness and safety. What elements made that moment special?

Mindful Walking: If you're in a cozy space allowing movement, take a slow, mindful walk. Focus on each step, feeling the ground beneath your feet and the rhythm of your body.

Cooking up a Storm: Reflect on a memorable meal shared with friends. What made it special?

Appreciation for Memories: Consider a favorite family tradition or holiday that evokes warmth. What made it special and how can you honor that memory now?

Snowy comfort: Recall a childhood memory of playing in the snow. What joy did that experience bring you?

Nature's Gifts: If you're surrounded by nature, list three things you appreciate about it – maybe the sounds, colors, or scents that enhance your cozy moment.

Act of Kindness: Recall a recent act of kindness you received. How did it make you feel, and why are you grateful for that person's gesture?

Movie Magic: Think about a movie that makes you feel empowered or uplifted. What messages or themes resonate with you?

Thankfulness for Skills: Reflect on a skill or talent you possess that brings you joy. How has this skill contributed to your sense of comfort or fulfillment?

Reading Reflection: Think of a book that changed your perspective. How has this book helped to enrich your life?

Mood Reflection: As you sit in your cozy moment, check in with your emotions. What are you feeling right now? Allow yourself to acknowledge and accept those feelings.

Reflect on support: Think of someone who makes your life feel cozier. What specific actions or qualities do they bring into your life that you're grateful for?

Mindful Eating: If you have a snack or drink, savor each bite or sip. Pay attention to the flavors, temperatures, and how they make you feel.

Seasonal Joys: Take a moment to appreciate the seasonal changes and the bounty of nature around you.

Joy in Simplicity: Reflect on a simple pleasure that made you smile today. It could be a lovely piece of music, a comforting scent, or a beautiful sunset.

Comforting creation: What comforts do you find in your creative hobbies? Reflect on the pleasure you experience by producing these items.

Supportive figures: Think of someone who has been a source of comfort in your life. Write down the specific ways they have supported you.

Embracing Solitude: Consider a solo moment that brought you peace. How does spending time alone nourish you?

Community Appreciation: Think about your community or neighborhood. What aspects make you feel connected and supported?

Thankfulness for Routine: Consider a daily routine that brings you comfort. How does this routine provide a sense of stability and coziness in your life?

Nature Observations: Observe the natural world if you can see outside. What changes do you notice in the environment? How do they enhance your cozy feeling?

Feel the Thrill: Envision the joy and exhilaration of sledding – the cold air, the speed and the laughter. Savor the thrill of the moment.

Gratitude for Silence: Spend a moment in silence. Notice how it feels to be alone with your thoughts and what that silence brings up for you.

Cozy Rituals: Think about a small ritual that brings you comfort (like brewing coffee or lighting a candle). How does it feel to engage in this action?

Healing Potions: Identify a natural remedy that has helped you. What do you appreciate about nature's healing power?

Cherish Memories: Recall a past cozy moment that stands out to you. What made it special, and how can you recreate that feeling now?

Yoga Joy: Reflect on your body and what it can do for you. What aspects of your physical self are you grateful for today?

Temperature Awareness: Pay attention to the temperature around you. Notice how the warmth of a blanket or a cup of coffee feels against your skin.

Cozy Coast: List three things you love about the coast—sounds, sights, or feelings. How do they enhance your experience?

Daily Comforts: What small comforts did you experience today? Consider things like a favorite meal, a warm shower, or a good book.

Gratitude for Creativity: Consider a creative outlet that brings you joy. How does engaging in this activity enhance your cozy moments

Warming Visualization: Imagine a warm light surrounding you. Picture it is filling you with peace and comfort, melting away any worries or stress